THE END OF
SPECTACLE

Books by Virginia Konchan

Short stories
Anatomical Gift

Chapbooks
That Tree Is Mine
Vox Populi

THE END OF
SPECTACLE

VIRGINIA KONCHAN

Carnegie Mellon University Press
Pittsburgh 2018

Acknowledgments

Grateful acknowledgment is made to the editors of the following publications in which these poems, or slightly altered versions thereof, first appeared:

The Believer: "American Gothic"
Boston Review: "It Is the Perpetual Today"
Cerise Press: "Albero Della Vita"
Columbia: A Journal of Literature and Art: "Coco Chanel at Prix de l'Arc de Triomphe"
Everyday Genius: "The Red Kerchief"
Forklift, Ohio: "Shostakovich's Fugues"
Handsome: "Annotating *Hiroshima mon amour*"
Hobart: "Dolores Haze in an Antiquarian Bookstore"
Memorious: "Karate Trophy," "Metempsychosis"
Michigan Quarterly Review: "The Point of View of Weather"
The Nervous Breakdown: "Elegy for Whitney Houston"
The New Republic: "Resurrection of John Keats"
The New Yorker: "Love Story," "The Rose-Way in Giverny"
The Offending Adam: "Dolores Haze Enters the 10th Grade," "Scheherazade"
PANK: "Heroic Couplet," "Aqualung," "Fairy Tale"
Poet Lore: "John Keats"
Requited: "Romance of the Hand and Thumb"
Rhino: "Zsa Zsa Gabor Learns to Read"
The Rumpus: "Zoo"
Sixth Finch: "Dolores Haze Disappears in a Kidney-Shaped Pool"
Third Coast: "Rorschach"
Waccamaw: "Serenade"
The Wallace Stevens Journal: "The Great Physician"
Western Humanities Review: "Façade"

The poem "O Noir" was selected by D. A. Powell for inclusion in *Best New Poets 2011*.

The poem "Zsa Zsa Gabor Learns to Read" was selected for a 2014 Illinois Arts Council Grant (nominated by the editors of *Rhino*).

Thank you to Gerald Costanzo, Connie Amoroso, and the wonderful team at Carnegie Mellon University Press, for supporting this book.

To the Vermont Studio Center, Ox-Bow, Banff Centre, and Scuola Internazionale di Grafica, thank you.

Profound thanks to Bridget Lowe, Caitlyn Doyle, Jennifer Moore, Kathleen Rooney, Kate Greenstreet, Stephanie Bolster, Lina Vitkauskas, Glenn Shaheen, Kristina Marie Darling, Andrew Zawacki, Catherine Theis, Tyler Mills, Brianna Noll, Annah Browning, Brooke Wonders, Tommy Zurhellen, Mary Biddinger, Anthony Madrid, Liz Countryman, Klara Du Plessis, Stephanie Kartalopoulos, Karen Schubert, Liz Hildreth, Samuel Mercier, Cathy Wagner, Allison Benis White, Christopher Salerno, Wyn Cooper, Lisa Fishman, and Cyrus Cassells, for sustaining conversations, reading, and friendship.

Deepest gratitude to the faculty with whom I worked at the University of Illinois at Chicago: Christina Pugh, Walter Benn Michaels, Jennifer Ashton, Mark Canuel, and Roger Reeves.

Finally, love and thanks to my family, and to my most ardent supporter, Michael Spleit.

Book design: Bronwyn Kuehler

Library of Congress Control Number 2017950739
ISBN 978-0-88748-631-9
Copyright © 2018 by Virginia Konchan
Printed and bound in the United States of America

10 9 8 7 6 5 4 3 2 1

Contents

I.

Fairy Tale

The view from this tower is all
effluvium and waste. And you

in your Brooks Brothers suit,
narrowed eyes and pursèd lips:

I wish to leave my fortune to the
as-yet-unborn, conjure up a pony

on a glittering chain. For my next
birthday party, I want everyone

dressed as if for masquerade.
When I am old enough to enjoy piles

of accumulated wealth I will be a bag
of clanking bones, an emerald the size

of a tumor on my conquering hand.
All hail my liquidity, an ampersand.

Façade

This is the house Frank built.
Evolved from the Queen Anne.
A unifying shingle surface
stretched like a skin over frame.
The steeply pitched roof
may be hipped, gable,
or gambrel: materiality
of brick, wood, or stone.
Which is to say, one
can ignore the book. One
can take up any number
of Revival styles. It's like
choosing between hues
of gold! The view from
the southerly window
occluded by that iridescent
pine, which gleams in all
seasons. One can hit the book,
dog its pages, throw it into
the sea. Its edges warp.
Like a severed animal,
its essential parts cry
out — no, back — to me.

Resurrection Lyric

In my dream, I ran you a bath
of sublime temperature,
poured in a rivulet of blue foam.
You never stepped in.
It was purely decorative,
like a scene at an open house
lit by a scented candle.
The house is conceptual,
an architectural display.
I pray for those who are lost,
if sitting motionless
and recalling the steep banks
of the quiet grotto's interior
can constitute prayer.
If the spine is an alphabet,
I remain on the low rung,
practicing my guttural moan.
Speak. Call the body back.
Roll away the stone.

Amor Fati

I took you to the place
of my grandfather's birth:
you took me, to yours.
We ate poached salmon.
You spoke German fluently,
the sound like clattering
utensils in a closed drawer.
Some days, an embrace
is like a handshake.
Some days, it's filled
with a voltage
that can kill.
You held my skull
in your strong hands,
saying, in earnest, my name.
And this is how a prayer
is born, among the reeds:
lissome as a song,
crying out, *let nothing
come between us.*
Crying out in vain.

On Dissonance

I.
Jabès, on the sea: "If the sea had no ears to hear the sea,
it would be a gray sea of death. It would be a mined sea
whose explosions would threaten the world in its
elephant memory."

II.
Historian Édouard Ganche: "Chopin's skin was very white,
his cheeks sunken. Even his ears showed a form particular
to consumptives." Teacher Józef Elsner: "I was reluctant
to constrain Chopin with narrow, academic rules, so as
to allow the young artist to mature according to his nature."

III.
George Sand's nickname for Chopin, while alive:
Beloved Little Corpse.

IV.
1831: Chopin learns, while traveling, that the November
Uprising against Russia had been crushed, and pours
blasphemies into a journal that he kept secret
to the end of his life. Biographer: "These torrential outcries
found musical expression in *Revolutionary Étude in C Minor*."

V.
Like Kafka, Chopin proposed marriage, but never wed.
Maria Wodzińska, dismissed from his life with quiet ceremony:
after placing her collected letters in an envelope,
he wrote across the seal *My Sorrow*.

VI.
1849: Chopin's Paris funeral, delayed for weeks.
Mozart's *Requiem*, the score he desired to accompany
the service, required female singers, then banned
from The Church of the Madeleine. Compromise
between Church and death wish: the female singers
could sing, but from behind a velvet curtain.

VII.
Major Innovations: sonata, nocturne, waltz, prelude.
Invention: ballade. Poet, be seated at the piano.
Strike the black, otherworldly chord.

The Academy

My pretty, my pretty, my sweet,
my sweet, there is nothing to eat
here but rocks and snow. Winter,
love, is an acquired taste. Ask
Penelope, weary before her mirror.
Ask—you are new to these parts.
So it is with great circumspection
that I ask you to disrobe and don
this robe, of ermine and pearl.
Now I will cut your throat.
Before I do, note the golden inlay
on this herringbone fork and knife.
The fat is the fat of decorative art.
The blood is the blood of the work.
Now sing.

Zsa Zsa Gabor Learns to Read

I touch the platinum helmet
of my head, call out to my daughter,

Constance Francesca.
In my bedroom closet

is a threadbare blouse
I purchased in Hungary.

I don it, tie a sash around my waist.
How does one represent thinking?

I am a European idyll.
Motherhood keeps me sane.

When Jesus appeared at the murky well
I was there with my five hundred husbands.

The blue volt of my illiteracy made manifest
in my butchering of the vowels in his name.

Coco Chanel at Prix de l'Arc de Triomphe

All hail the end
of spectacle, pieces

of *royaume* scattered
on the sidewalk,

evolution of *la langue,*
after the fall of Paris,

from garbage
to decorative art.

Nurse, I want to get to the end
of the story, the song.

I want a final death
in my bolero jacket,

poised in my front-row
loge seat, accepting

the violence of the
track: hooves pounding,

dust flying, emcee
roaring, life-wound

of becoming-object
badly sutured by a quack

doctor on the plane to nowhere,
where I am instructed to enjoy,

beatifically, the end
of the sensible world.

Zoo

Unbridled, the sick pony
traverses listlessly a circle.
Something something about
the indifference of crows.
Nature draws a crowd:
amateur photographers
drawn to the ellipsis
of weather, the dew point
of sumac and wisteria vines.
Cross the sturdy footbridge;
greet the slack-jawed child.
Do not tell me this is not
beautiful, the clay heart
of Nature in the throes
of inconsequence, before
its animation by mind.

Corpus Christi

Dear ganglion. Dear aorta.
Dear progenitor. Dear nerve.

Dear darling lady in your pencil
skirt, your skittish laughter,

like an emergency brake
applied to the nonevent

of history, turns me on.
Dear one of helter-skelter

lifestyle choices and
even worse, *savoir-faire*:

you treat your body like the
common ancestor it is.

Dear gray matter.
Dear black matter.

Dear hurdy-gurdy of memory,
drawing us back, and in.

Dear memory of romance,
perfume stopper

longing for its *objet perdu*,
Chanel No. 5, 4, 3, or 2.

In the air, there your root remains, in the air.
I shudder without theater or jest, for you.

Love Story

My body has never been my body.
It has been a bucket of asphalt
upside down in the puerile wind.
My horse faltered at the finish line.
I whipped it and it plunged forth,
like froth on the crest of a wave.
My horse is my body: my body,
my horse. Slick flank, waxen
hair—do not bother to do
the math. My mouth is full
of epithet; my horse is fat
and tame. Touch me.
Announce yourself.
Now is the heroic age.

II.

Vita Nova

Hell, too, is dialectic.
Marrying to every word a twinborn sigh.

Your body is a segment of prehistoric road.
A buried stairwell with only the top stair obvious.

Who tells of the place where the sun rests?
Who foretells the ages of the moon?

I gaze through a telescope at the Orion Nebula,
blue vapor with a cluster of white stars.

Aloneness is the first hygienic measure.
Without, our shame: within, our consciences.

Do you notice anything foreign in me?
My suffering has disappeared.

Punctus Contra Punctum

The butcher's wife's death was messy.
People moaned. It was a *wait stop* death,
a *now I love you* death, yet was deliberate,

slow, in the collapsed space between what
one imagines might happen (a reprieve) and
what is actually happening (a bludgeoning).

Wordsworth was right: dissection is for fools,
and painting by numbers will always be a lesser
art. Did you nail the kiss of death, the ghost

of Rachmaninoff asked the butcher, in his dreams. The
resounding chord, was it ivory, or, white? *Monsignor,*
he replied, *before the desire for meaning gave birth*

to music, and the desire for death, to refinement
of mind, it was not difficult, but merely impossible,
to hold a note that trembled in the highest key of C.

Elegy for Whitney Houston

It's a matter of not coming back
when you say you won't come back,
of dousing the fire luck and happenstance
made. The reaper turned out to be lively,
tossing out ripostes like burgers at
a fundraiser for teens. O deliquescent one.
I hold you the way one rides
a mechanical bull, a good grip
and a wave of bandana besides.
The echo chamber is in flames, Whitney,
the think tank, too, and we are asked
to skip merrily through the parade.
That I could spur you: that I could wake
you: that I could call you and that you
would answer by any other name.

Shostakovich's Fugues

Lunch is roast beef on ghastly onion buns.
I abstain, icon of sublime indifference,
feasting on devil-may-care-duende
from a Russian madman in the
tonic key of C major instead:
atonal language of soma
and brute infant cries.
Dear demonology,
I want to be free
from hebephiles, slave labor,
and shrunken miniskirts.
Dmitri, I too failed the exam
in Marxist methodology:
the glass-walled *Conservatoire*
won't house, or save, us now.

Scheherazade

The moment I stop
laying golden eggs
at your feet, meat
of legal tender,
sonic wallpaper
of place and thing
(floating signifiers
of your trash-strewn,
transitive soul), you die.
1001 nights: how long,
in the chain mail of history,
I didn't exist save as cipher:
matrix of guillotined tongue.
You: propped on sultan pillows.
Me: matter-turned-*spiritus*,
dissolving in crenellated air.

American Gothic

I.
Regionalist painter Thomas Hart Benton was naturally stunned
by the commercial success of his pupil Jackson Pollock,
whose *No. 5, 1948*, a "nest-like drizzle of yellows and browns
on fiberboard," sold for 140 million, becoming the most
expensive painting in the history of modern art, and this,
after the (near) seduction of his one wife Rita!
Pollock: *"She was the ideal woman."*

II.
Childhood: hunger. His mother Stella, strangely inexpressive:
"She sat like statuary the entire evening and didn't move once."
Romantic History: his approach with Lee Krasner, after
formal introductions at a dinner party: "Do you like to fuck?"

III.
Mentor: "He couldn't absorb words and he couldn't use them,
but he picked up on the subtlest nonverbal signals."
Protégé: "Dammit, Tom, dammit! You know what I mean!"

IV.
Verbs used to describe Pollock's process of applying paint:
fling, dribble, hurl, and *dump*

(*drip* having become the name of the style).

V.
Art Historian: "None of Pollock's paintings are true abstractions.
They are fundamentally figurative paintings, albeit in a way
that's hard to read."

VI.
Reporter: "So, Jack, how does it feel to be considered the father
of Abstract Expressionism?"
Pollock: "What the hell is Abstract Expressionism?"

VII.

1943: Compositional space of *Mural*: a barn. Technique: two days spent crawling over a thirty-foot canvas, flinging cigarette ash, paint, and glue. (Bio. note: He wrote *Jackson Pollock* across the canvas, then hung the imagery from the letters of his name.)

The Red Kerchief

after Monet

Lightning zigzags across a starlit sky,
but I am stone cold, no, colder

than stone. My Paleolithic heart
blooms through the blackness

of attire. I am dressed for market,
to buy items for our brood.

You see me as if through glass:
it is the face, now aged, you once

cradled and adored. The poplar parts,
revealing the sapling of a poplar,

dendritic diagram. It is winter:
has been, will be.

I am not appeased by the mere
suggestion of movement, reality.

It Is the Perpetual Today

The pool is empty; no bathers stand nearby.
The beast must be glorified and so each bristle stands out
on its raised, humped back.

The pool must be glorified and so each aquamarine tile glistens,
having been scrubbed, before the photograph was taken,
with bleach.

It is the perpetual today, that which has historians running
through empty fields in white coats,
taking the pulse of the world . . .

The beast breathes silently, exhaling steam from its nostrils.
The crowd maintains its distance and its composure:
how like a crowd.

The beast maintains its beastliness: how like a beast.
That which is wild will remain wild.

The last doctrine is that of redistribution of matter.
The last item is a stick, and, at the end of the stick,
a soul.

Sans Soleil

Children of Iceland, listen well
to your future progeny:
the funnel cakes you eat
at the carnival in Guinea-
Bissau are not, in the last
assessment, connected
to the ferry that ferried
you from Hokkaido to
Antigua Bay.
Camels petrified
by desert drought:
teens dancing
in a public square:
this was the miscellany
of a new millennium,
one that once had,
as I did, time to spare.
The girls of Cape
Verde comb their
hair carefully,
as well they should.
He wrote me.
He wrote me.
The end of war is
its own love affair.

Dolores Haze in an Antiquarian Bookstore

Persona non grata, I slouch against
wood paneled décor, my fuchsia nails
thumbing through the sorcery of Montesquieu.
Can I help you, asks the gnarly old man, his life
spent within the hoary cover of a textile factory,
protected, or rather shielded, from public view.
I cannot afford to buy Edmund Spenser's
"THE FAERIE QUEEN" (London, 1751:
3-vol. set, quarto. 1st English Edition,
original calf & gilt bindings: $12,500).
I instead buy the BRUCE LEE
collection: 67 different magazines
featuring his 1990s prowess.
All clean. Pile one foot tall.
I walk out that much broker,
wanting to have bought each
RARE JEM, as advertised.
What care I for karate?
The gulf between desire
and means will be
the death of us all.

Dolores Haze Disappears in a Kidney-Shaped Pool

I stand at the diving platform,
goggles fixed, waiting for the sound
of the pistol shot, the slapping noise
of teenage bodies going aqueous,
thrashing their way into form.
After the meet, the girls turban
their hair, stomp around with
pixelated eyes and sturdy thighs,
before going for pizza. Jesus,
the mundane life shimmers
like an oasis to my felon
heart, made black
in fealty to my lord.

Dolores Haze As a Bildungsroman

No nymph in bobby socks,
blue-shadowed eyes rolling
with adolescent churlishness:
the electric eel of Circe's rage
courses like spit through
my veins. Analog to your
allegory, hovel to your
abattoir, Polaroid to your
lowbrow decorative frieze,
I learned patience for the
second sex sorting M&M's
by color while Presley crooned
"Viva Las Vegas" on my screen.
On my wall: a wedding photo
of Jerry Lee Lewis and his bride.
I curtsy prettily in the mirror,
biding my time: this mask
has a hole for a mouth.

Dolores Haze Enters the 10th Grade

I open my clenched fists,
breathe in atomized air:
keening for the whistle
of the kettle, train, or inner ear.
The man I fled and toward whom
I'm walking, with purposeful gait,
are not the same man. To one
I was datum, flesh, a beast
to harness for a life
on a racetrack, circling
madly at impossible speeds.
To the other I am human,
quiet in my orbit, and clean.
I shut the door to the boudoir
with reluctance, open geometry:
chicken scratch whose formal logic
I will, to be worthy of love, endeavor
to understand, master, or believe.

The Rose-Way in Giverny

after Monet

And in the reticulate distance
the cued inertia of Lucifer
astounds. Our feet bleed:
buoyant, the body at its task.
What you wanted was what I
wanted — slant of sun to the left,
twinkling of civilization elsewise,
and the moon (whelp of history)
to our backs, all come-hither
and dream. Motion understood
is philosophy deferred: peace,
the felt pathos of space and time.
Look, darling, at the establishing
shot. It's downright biblical,
this thrown-together vista,
world upon world without end.

III.

The Point of View of Weather

after Virginia Woolf

1.
Perfect Day. Evening fine so we went
out again into the hollow. Saw a shining spot,
which we could not see when we came up to it.
Painted Lady *[Vanessa cardui]* seen near Glynde.
A threshing machine at work, behind the wood.

2.
L. planted Japanese anemones on the terrace. Guns heard.
A thoroughly bad day from the point of view of weather.
Carrying my manuscript to *The Times* I felt like a hack.
We left it with a porter, who flourished his hat. Lilian:
most modest & resolute. Aldous Huxley: long & lean.

3.
Bert is wounded. I left Alix to her sepulchral despair. Windows
are broken according to no rule; not much gossip about the King.
He prefers mad Princess Victoria. His head is smooth as an egg.
Hardly grumbled today, though it was inhuman, primeval weather.
Day spent recumbent. Melancholy letter from Ott., complaining of age.

4.
A party—Mr. Lock (with some impediment) was there, & Flora,
& Clara & Sylvia—malice suggesting the whole of Kensington
High Street poured into a room. "Oh! Ah! How splendid,"
everyone cried, as if on stage. Most strange is why Nature
has produced this type in such abundance. Faith vacillated about,
endeavoring to make me see her show of dresses.

5.
K. broke with Ott., in a letter which says, "You shant play Countess
to my cook." Lady Strachey: eyes collapsed, teeth gone. Arnold
outdid me in antinationalism. Saturday: Kew. Snowdrops,
dwarf cyclamen, miniature rhododendrons, coming through the
dead leaves. Figaro, at the Old Vic. The vindication of opera!
I was asked to write a book: "Makers of the 19th Century."
After deliberation, I refused.

Albero Della Vita

When you deny me, the world denies me.
I am embraced by a canopy of skulls.
Cornflowers wheel through open space,
spindly things in inhospitable terrain.
I am seeking the limit you embody,
bodiless, a changeling whose name
in a different alphabet means *like*.
Vegetation is not love, is not life:
it is the pleasure god takes in an
onrush of green. I mark the days
on a calendar of fertility, sip
densely sugared mint tea.
Crawl toward me, beloved.
I am the earth and the sea.

John Keats

The crashing of wave against shore in Margate
was a metaphor for the drama of delimitation,
but when has it not been so? The name

of my childhood god in Moorgate was
I am that I am—dying. It's not difficult.
Let me be plain. I tore an aphid, newly

bloomed, apart with my two bare hands
in Hampstead. I perfected sentiment,
then perfected it some more. The tumor

of my black lyric, too, bloomed, fixation
both in and of this world, unlike you,
dream of transcendence, against which

I struggle, and the reason for my killing
of your kind. After the aphid, I turned
on others a chemical spray. What I did

not destroy in open air I did in secret, yes,
I opened the bud's mouth—it did not resist,
for this I give thanks—and angled poison in.

Dead Metaphor

Fiction can sustain
the hypotactic,
composite phrase.
But I am a poem,
Lord, flyaway
cowlick on the
forehead of
preindustrial
man, singing
Stille, mein wille!
I rise, octopi ink
streaming from
once-webbed
hands, to write you
a letter thanking you
for capturing, flaying,
then releasing me,
fish gutted,
to the land.

Resurrection of John Keats

First, brace yourself. The romantic is back,
feet propped, convalescing from the fiction
of an interventionist god. Tough journey.
Long. Oxymoronic lovechild of nature
and art, tell it slant on that red guitar:

that nightingale is not a bird. It's a folio
of Homer, a cash cow on fire. So notch up
your amulet of pain, living hand lanced,
then outstretched. Clearance finally given
to the lover, who, outfitted with a conscience,

heretofore dead (how like a god), has just spoken
the world's first sentence, distinct as a hiccup,
in response to the tubercular prognosis: *Hello*.
O Hyperion, Fanny breathed, this is *that* new.
Beauty ungovernable, m'lord, because true.

O Noir

Hell is following as if drugged.
To your left, a curtain: to your right, a door.

The woman is blind. She thumps on the door
mechanically, twice, to confirm its presence.

You are led to the table of rhetoric.
Its edges are beveled and smooth.

The food you've ordered in advance
arrives: crème brûlée and aubergines.

You can't find it with your fork
and the stranger accompanying you

can't see you eat it, nor can anyone else.
You scoop it into your mouth like water.

These are the pleasantries of hell, and these, the consolations:
soft laughter, the scraping of chairs.

This is hell's ambiance and you are its ambassador:
faceless, lucent, reduced to proximity and touch.

Your eyes—bloodshot vessels—cast around
for a fixed point or a vanishing point in vain:

they've become the same thing.
You tell the stranger you love him.

You tell the stranger you hate him.
You ask: what kind of egg is this?

The stranger shrugs, says *quail*.
Your waitress announces her appearance:

"I am beside you, Gloria."
You must remind her that is not your name.

You stand to make a speech about this ordeal
because that—speech—is the parlance of hell,

and out of your star mouth
tumbles inconsequential music

in·perfect four-four time, to which,
after a spell, the stranger rolls his eyes and says,

Not here, not now.

Mary Shelley

You are the furthest thing
from a Pre-Raphaelite painting
I know. Your middle man
a monster, you wake at midnight,
candles ablaze, remembering
the last line you wrote, then
the line that came before.
Your heathen love a creature
standing eight feet tall:
jaundiced skin, steel
piping through his neck.
You spent your life beside
rivers with impossible names —
Thames, Serpentine.
You invented the inventor.
You escaped debtor's prison.
Suicide is not an option anymore.

The Great Physician

Spring's bright paradise has come to this.
The stethoscope of the sun is on my breast.

The string that holds me is crazed and flayed.
I hold a leash, but there is no dog.

A myth is not a fact. It's a haystack, Canada
stuck beneath. *I still exist*, she whispers

to the crowd. When the fog lifted, I took
a tugboat out to sea, and married it. The sea.

Apart from that, Wellbutrin steers me
through the shipyard of sleep. Aphasic,

I languish on an operation table. Doctor
thinks the unwell soul is a machine.

Metempsychosis

This is the dance of no hard feelings,
deranged sonnet constructed
to resemble a paper Valentine.
All morning the mother animal
refused to nurse the baby animal,
whether a mongoose, seal, or sea
urchin, birthed on wind-whipped
horizons stacked with travelers'
skulls. I don a red woolen cap,
keep going. The arctic elements
hurl insults before relenting.
The crowd's collective sullen
face: dust on a spiral staircase
overlaid with ice, or gold.

Dwarf Morning Glory

Beauty is as beauty does,
balm for the garbage disposal
of commodity cycles'
ventricular windows,
opening only at dawn.
So too, diurnal bloom
of this ipomoea tricolor:
blue-white trumpets
marked with a darker
blue star. Ideal for
trellis, fence, obelisk —
five points shoot out
from its white throat.
When I die, I feign,
Lady Shalott, sleep:
rising to bend mind's
blown fuse around *énoncé,*
intercellular choreography
of the impossible, *to speak.*

Heroic Couplet

It's no use. The starry flock has come and gone.
In its place, tractor trailers, the ever-dying dawn.

Mise en garde: a lone red crayon,
demented plastic cup.

A stranger on the verandah,
corsage in trembling hand.

All my skills, I'm learning,
in hell, are secretarial.

I am floating in a sea of painkillers,
bent awkwardly, like a suitor, at the knee.

I await your wide white sash:
classical sign of clemency.

Incunabula

It's tax season on my
devotional altar,
pseudoscience of
a High Latin Mass:
write-offs include
worry dolls and incense,
doxa of overthrown gods
(stimulus and scarcity,
supply and demand).
Beyond the Pater Noster
dissolving in the cradle
endlessly rocking, now
stilled, remains my body:
aegis of the invisible hand
outstretched, crowning
touch the fontanel,
spyware protected,
of the name.

Aqualung

I have not been in rehab
or prison or to a kibbutz.

I am invisible to rain.
I want only something

strange and beautiful:
a heart oplayod by a

knife, a kiddie pool
filled with bubbles,

odor of conifers
in a great room

occupied by you,
your bluish hair,

and your 10,000-
foot bridal train.

Serenade

That there should be ceremony.
A way into the photo album
before sepia became *de rigueur*.
That there should be upright collars,
a flower on the mantel as a timepiece.
In this way the flower does not differ
from the camera itself, from the lucidity
of the operative lens with its shuttlecock
eye, closing when done after recording
the blurred colors of transient things.
I dream of Ruth, stock-still amid the corn.
I dream you, your staff laid waste
on fertile soil. That there should be fruit.
That it should be proffered and initially
refused. That paradise should pile
up on your ship, oranges at the helm
of the bodhisattva's sumptuous robe.
But before union, leave-taking.
The gondolier idles in queue.
The last tremolo string of the principal
cellist should convey, *sotto voce*,
I was commissioned for you.

IV.

Immaculate Conception

Come play, he said. You can be the horse.
It was a mating dance of signals and
scripts. We ate unripened plums.

He knelt, offered his hand. A wife at 13?
Inconceivable. My face, impervious,
closed. I lowered it into the ground.

No flowers grew in our untilled soil.
But how could I abandon the manifesto
of destiny? He twitched with passion,

cursed the continental divide.
The wind, restless, pounded the sky
like an ape. Yesterday, I saw him,

held my head up high. The idea
of freedom! Someone leapt:
someone else was dragged.

Nativity Scene

after Gauguin

Loosened upon a canary divan,
within a thatched hut

in a village beside the sea.
I have a foothold in consciousness,

yet am possessed by the idea of none.
Thus, ocean breezes.

Thus, the molten purr
of a kitten at my knee.

My wet nurse is near,
with my infant in arms.

Search not, art critic, for the moral lesson
—famine, fire, flood—in this frame.

Dear Platonic duality, the broken object
in this painting is not my body, it is me.

Bat Anatomy

It's the marsupial
that does the most for me,

but bat: do not become
discouraged.

You have been inverted
for 10,000 years. Your
night vision is bar none.

Insects are a delicacy?
Bat, it's you who are
the forbidden fruit:

covered in must,
screeching. Come now,
show me the flawless

seam in your wing.
Make pentecostal
the argument from design.

Karate Trophy

Sociability occurs
to one like the idea of god:
humped camel on the horizon
lurching forth on hindquarters,
all unmet need and malaise.
That's me in the corner,
jealously guarding my
little chrome tower.
I am swimming in a red
pantsuit, winding up for
shuto uchi, uke waza.
Anything to prove
that I am more than
body: or that that
body, a machine,
has been raised.

Annotating Hiroshima mon amour

I'd rather be reading Lucretius—
who, according to St. Jerome,
was driven mad by a love philter,
wrote poetry in lucid intervals,
and died by his own hand.
All lies. That's what I get
for placing gold coins atop
the shut eyes of the gaze:
a 36-hour film starring
Emmanuelle Riva
and Eiji Okada. *I loved
the taste of blood since
tasting yours, Elle*
confesses to *Il*. God
names only to condemn . . .
Bureaucracy's final rapture:
beyond human love,
a paradise-turned-
spectacle of forms.

Anodyne

There is no cure for passion,
nor poverty, save for shillings
pouring forth from urns
at the defunct church:
ashes of saints and minions,
unaware that history
is a game in which we are
played like wind instruments
from 14th century France,
broken on the knee of churls,
then painstakingly repaired
by the world's last luthier.
You play at the dulcimer
to a harem of nymphets
while I walk upon water,
causal reality a makeshift
stage for your plebiscite
resurrection, death of
the spectacle (and spectrality)
leaving us clutching
ticket stubs, then each
other, at the carnival's
exit gate, too broke,
or astonished, to feel.

Romance of the Hand and Thumb

It is a pity it is evening, Li Po:
would that we could all sit,
cracking brazil nuts and
muckraking with the moon.
And yet look! The supinated
limbs of factory laborers, sewing
buttons onto starched shirts until
nimble fingers dehisce, reattach
to wrists, arms, then torsos:
sensations stir, a cool breeze.
Tell a dream, lose a reader:
how else to explain Daphne's
rebellion from the god of
sex: rights reverting, after
the production of desire,
to you, and me, and trees.

Rorschach

Goodbye, starboard.
Goodbye, feral kitten in a box by the sea.
I like the feel of this sanatorium.
Its walls are papered with orange moons
and rakish persimmons, once blighted,
now ripe. On the subject of paranoid
hallucinations: the body of my brother
is crippled and Christ-like. A tin can
communication device is stretched
between us, though the distance be
the stuff of reverie. With regard
to the visual field, I see the crossed
eyes of a former rival divided out
in the constellated field above me.

Madonna and Child

It took place, the dream,
within a mind no wider

than a fist: but the subject
is no longer subject. Duccio,

the artist who froze her
using, what, another picture?

for inspiration. Ideas are things.
And things don't fare much better.

Just yesterday, the baby opened
an eye. *Who are you?* he asked

of Mary. The icon, she said. Hush.
The illusion is almost complete.

Notes

The line "In the air, there your root remains, in the air," in the poem "Corpus Christi," is borrowed from Paul Celan.

The cento "Vita Nova" includes text from Anne Boyer, John Keats, Robin Coste Lewis, Amairgen, Arthur Sze, Anna Swir, George Herbert, and Lynn Xu.

"The Point of View of Weather" borrows and reassembles language from the five published volumes of Virginia Woolf's diary.

The German excerpt in the poem "Dead Metaphor" (*"Stille, mein wille!"*) is from the poem "Stille, mein wille!" (Be still, my soul!) by Katharina von Schlegel, 1752.

The line "This is the dance of no hard feelings" in the poem "Metempsychosis" is borrowed from Mark Bibbins' poetry collection *The Dance of No Hard Feelings*.

The first five lines of "Annotating *Hiroshima, Mon Amour*" are taken from the *Stanford Encyclopedia of Philosophy*'s entry for Titus Lucretius Carus, an Epicurean poet of the late Roman republican era, best known for the six-book Latin hexameter poem *De rerum natura* (*On the Nature of Things*).

Photo: Michael Spleit

Virginia Konchan is the author of a short story collection, *Anatomical Gift* (Noctuary Press, 2017), and two chapbooks, *That Tree Is Mine* (dancing girl press, 2017), and *Vox Populi* (Finishing Line Press, 2015). Her poetry has appeared in *The New Yorker*, *The New Republic*, *Best New Poets*, *Boston Review*, and elsewhere.